AMERICAN VALUES AND FREEDOMS

THE RIGHT TO
VOTE

by DUCHESS HARRIS, JD, PHD with Kari A. Cornell

Essential Library

An Imprint of Abdo Publishing | abdopublishing.com

ABDOPUBLISHING.COM

Published by Abdo Publishing, a division of ABDO, PO Box 398166, Minneapolis, Minnesota 55439. Copyright © 2018 by Abdo Consulting Group, Inc. International copyrights reserved in all countries. No part of this book may be reproduced in any form without written permission from the publisher. Essential Library™ is a trademark and logo of Abdo Publishing.

Printed in the United States of America, North Mankato, Minnesota
102017
012018

Interior Photos: Bettmann/Getty Images, 4–5, 21, 33; AP Images, 8, 11; Everett Collection/Newscom, 13; Joseph Sohm/Shutterstock Images, 16–17; Hulton Archive/Archive Photos/Getty Images, 18; Library of Congress, 23, 30, 31, 40; Everett Historical/Shutterstock Images, 24, 42, 44–45, 49; Alfred R. Waud/Harper's Weekly/Library of Congress, 28; Harris & Ewing/Library of Congress, 39; MPI/Archive Photos/Getty Images, 47; McD/AP Images, 51; Horace Cort/AP Images, 54; Dozier Mobley/AP Images, 58–59; Ron Sachs/picture-alliance/dpa/AP Images, 63; Dave Martin/AP Images, 64; Eric Gay/AP Images, 66–67; P. Kevin Morley/Richmond Times-Dispatch/AP Images, 70; Red Line Editorial, 73, 80; Terry Evans/TNS/Newscom, 74; Tom Williams/CQ Roll Call/AP Images, 76; Steve Helber/AP Images, 83; Ron Sachs/CNP/AdMedia/Newscom, 86–87; Ryan J. Foley/AP Images, 90; D. Netrom Photos/Shutterstock Images, 94; Eddie Moore/ZumaPress/Newscom, 96

Editor: Marie Pearson
Series Designer: Becky Daum

Publisher's Cataloging-in-Publication Data

Names: Harris, Duchess, author. | Cornell, Kari A., author.
Title: The right to vote / by Duchess Harris and Kari A. Cornell.
Description: Minneapolis, Minnesota : Abdo Publishing, 2018. | Series: American values and freedoms | Online resources and index.
Identifiers: LCCN 2017946729 | ISBN 9781532113048 (lib.bdg.) | ISBN 9781532151927 (ebook)
Subjects: LCSH: Suffrage–United States–Juvenile literature. | United States–Politics and government–Juvenile literature. | Voting–Juvenile literature. | Constitutional law–United States–Juvenile literature.
Classification: DDC 324.6209–dc23
LC record available at https://lccn.loc.gov/2017946729

CONTENTS

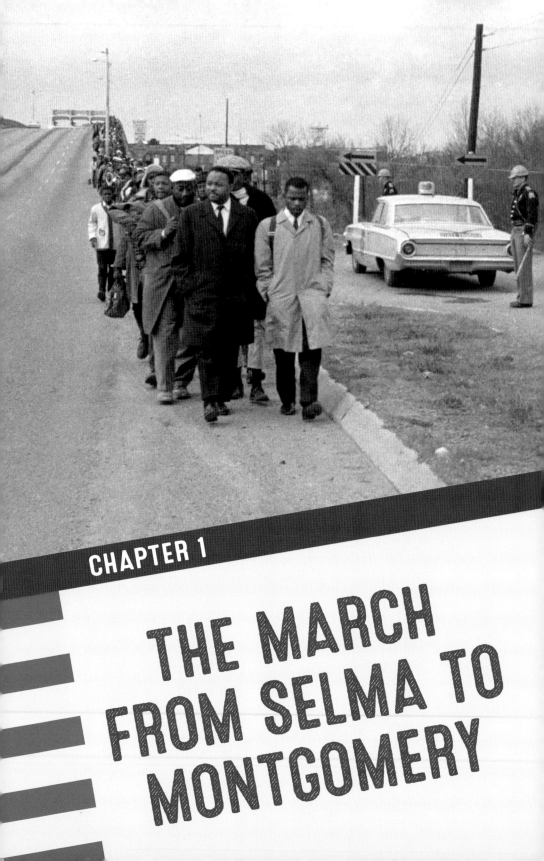

CHAPTER 1

THE MARCH FROM SELMA TO MONTGOMERY

A long history of injustice in Selma inspired people to march for change on March 7, 1965.

Early in the morning on Sunday, March 7, 1965, African Americans began gathering at the Brown Chapel African Methodist Episcopal (AME) Church in Selma, Alabama. Although they would attend a Sunday service, most of the congregants did not come to hear the sermon. On this day, they would begin the 54-mile (87 km) march to the state capitol in Montgomery in the name of voting rights. For three years, civil rights activists had worked without success to register African Americans to vote. This march was the next step in the struggle, and it promised to be dangerous.

As the 600 marchers left the chapel at 1:40 p.m. and headed toward the Edmund Pettus Bridge, their moods were somber.[1] Hosea Williams of the Southern Christian Leadership Conference (SCLC) and John Lewis and Robert Mants, members of the Student Nonviolent Coordinating Committee (SNCC, pronounced "snick"), led the march. They'd warned the marchers that Alabama state troopers would likely use tear gas to stop them. The police would have billy clubs and other weapons, and there would be dogs. If the police put them under arrest, the marchers knew what to do: They were to kneel down, tuck their heads between their knees, and place their hands over their heads. They were not to resist arrest.

JIMMIE LEE JACKSON

Of the 600 activists who marched in Selma on March 7, 1965, many came from the nearby town of Marion, Alabama. They marched in honor of Jimmie Lee Jackson. Three weeks earlier, on February 18, these same activists had participated in a peaceful night march to protest the arrest of activist and SCLC member James Orange. But things had gotten out of hand. Police had turned off the streetlights and had begun hunting down and beating African-American protesters. Police chased some of the protesters, including 26-year-old church deacon Jimmie Lee Jackson, into Mack's Café. While protecting his mother and grandfather from the police, Jackson was shot in the stomach. He died eight days later at Good Samaritan Hospital in Selma. His death inspired the Selma to Montgomery march.

MARCHING IN FEAR

Albert Turner, one of the marchers, remembered the fear he felt that day. "We really thought we were going to get killed. I ain't lying, every step I made that Sunday, I trembled. We knew we were walking into hell."[2]

When the marchers reached the middle of the bridge, the wall of 200 Alabama state troopers and police officers, standing several deep, came into view. The sight of them— many on horseback, wearing helmets, and carrying clubs and bullwhips—caused Williams, Lewis, and Mants to stop in their tracks. Clearly, the police were ready for battle.

As the marchers approached the police, Major John Cloud ordered them to turn around and go back to their churches. Instead, the marchers knelt and bowed their heads to pray. The troops responded by stepping forward and charging toward the marchers, tossing grenades filled with tear gas into the crowd. A few hundred white spectators began to cheer on the officers. As the tear gas took effect, the marchers tried to make their way back across the bridge to the chapel, sometimes stumbling over others as they struggled to see. Many marchers jumped off the bridge and into the Alabama River to avoid the tear gas. But the troopers pursued the marchers, hitting them with clubs and trying to trample them with the horses. More than 50 people were hospitalized for their injuries, including Lewis, who suffered a fractured skull, and Amelia Boynton Robinson, founder of the Dallas County Voters League, who was beaten unconscious.[3] The day would go down in history as "Bloody Sunday."

A NATION OUTRAGED

Within two days, protests against the violent attacks on the marchers in Selma broke out in 80 US cities.[4] Citizens made

State troopers beat protesters including John Lewis, *kneeling*, with billy clubs on Bloody Sunday.

calls and sent telegrams to the White House, imploring President Lyndon B. Johnson to do something to protect the African-American marchers. Activists from all over the country traveled to Alabama to lend their support to the movement. Religious leaders, including Rev. Martin Luther King Jr., rushed to Selma as well. But they were not allowed to march. Federal judge Frank Johnson Jr. had issued a temporary restraining order, prohibiting anyone involved from taking further action before he could review the case.

But with so many activists arriving from out of town, King believed some action must be taken. He and other civil rights leaders feared that if they did nothing, the cause would lose momentum. President Johnson had sent Assistant Attorney General John Doar and US Community Relations Committee director LeRoy Collins to reach a compromise with local law enforcement. King would be allowed to march, and the police

CAPTURED ON CAMERA

As police beat marchers with clubs in the yellow tear-gas haze, journalists from ABC News snapped photos and shot video. ABC News interrupted the showing of *Judgment in Nuremberg*, a documentary about Nazi war crimes during World War II (1939–1945), to air the footage from the Selma march. The scenes of Alabama police wading through the crowd and aggressively beating African-American marchers shocked the nation.

promised not to attack the activists. So on March 9, King led supporters on a march from the Brown Chapel to the site of the attacks at the Edmund Pettus Bridge. But instead of marching on, the protesters knelt down to pray. Then King announced they would peacefully return to the church.

THE MOVEMENT MUST CONTINUE

Although the second symbolic march was peaceful, the civil rights activists suffered another devastating blow later that evening. While returning to the Brown Chapel after dinner, James Reeb, Orloff Miller, and Rev. Clark Olsen, three clergymen in town for the march, took a wrong turn and walked past the Silver Moon Café, a restaurant frequented by members of the Ku Klux Klan (KKK). This group did not want African Americans to have the same rights as white people and it sometimes used violence. A group of white men from the café approached Reeb, Miller, and Olsen from behind, muttering racial slurs. Then one of the men hit Reeb on the left side of the head with a lead pipe. The next day, Reeb died of a massive brain injury.

Reeb's death gave the civil rights activists in Selma and the rest of the nation another reason to continue their fight. On March 21, 1965, with the consent of Alabama judge Frank Johnson, King once again led a group of civil rights marchers

Demonstrators hold a vigil for Reeb in Selma on March 11.

DR. MARTIN LUTHER KING JR.

Dr. Martin Luther King Jr. fought tirelessly to extend the right to vote to all Americans. To King, the right to vote was the very foundation of citizens' ability to think for themselves and participate fully in the democratic process. King believed that if any part of society was denied the right to vote on reaching adulthood, the government itself was compromised. How could the government expect those who had no voice in representation or the laws of the land to willingly follow those laws? By denying African Americans the right to vote, King proclaimed, the government was ignoring the very principles of an honest democracy. If given the right to vote, African Americans would have the power to elect legislators to represent their concerns. As a means to this end, King led voting rights activists in Selma in nonviolent demonstrations to bring national attention to discrimination against African Americans at polling booths throughout the South. Thanks to King's leadership, the Voting Rights Act became a reality.

from the Brown Chapel in Selma toward the Edmund Pettus Bridge. This time, the marchers had the protection of National Guard troops sent by President Johnson. Thousands of marchers—African American and white, male and female, young and old—began the trek to Montgomery.

On this day, when the marchers reached the other side of the Alabama River, no state troopers blocked their path. Throughout the four-day march, volunteers provided the activists with food. When night fell, the marchers unpacked

Protesters cross the Edmund Pettus Bridge on March 21.

THE AMERICAN PROMISE

President Johnson addressed Congress on the evening of March 15, 1965, delivering what came to be called his "American Promise" speech. In it, the president made a pledge to restore voting rights to African Americans. He said, "The Constitution says that no person shall be kept from voting because of his race or his color. We have all sworn an oath before God to support and to defend that Constitution. We must now act in obedience to that oath. Wednesday I will send to Congress a law designed to eliminate illegal barriers to the right to vote."[7] With these words, President Johnson launched legislation that would lead to the passing of the Voting Rights Act of 1965.

bedrolls and slept in fields along Highway 80. By the time the group reached the capitol in Montgomery, its numbers had swelled to 25,000.[5] At last, they had arrived.

THE VOTING RIGHTS ACT OF 1965

As a direct result of the Selma-to-Montgomery march, President Johnson signed the Voting Rights Act into law on August 6, 1965. The act outlawed the use of literacy tests at voter registration centers. The law also provided federal representatives to monitor voter registration in parts of the country where less than half of the minority population had registered to vote. Under this historic act, the number of African-American voters increased significantly. In 1966, 450,000 African Americans had registered to vote.[6]

The Voting Rights Act was a monumental step in securing enfranchisement for all Americans. Yet even today, the struggle to make sure state laws abide by the Voting Rights Act continues. Biased redistricting threatens to limit voters' influence, while voter identification (ID) laws prevent some Americans from voting at all. In fact, the Voting Rights Act itself has been challenged in the Supreme Court as an outdated law that is no longer needed. The fight to guarantee voting rights is far from over.

DISCUSSION STARTERS

- Do you believe the civil rights activists did the right thing by marching across the Edmund Pettus Bridge in March 1965? Why or why not?

- Have you ever witnessed or been the target of discrimination? If so, how did you react?

- Do you think King's peaceful approach to protest was effective? Why or why not?

- How did the police reaction to the Selma protesters affect the civil rights movement?

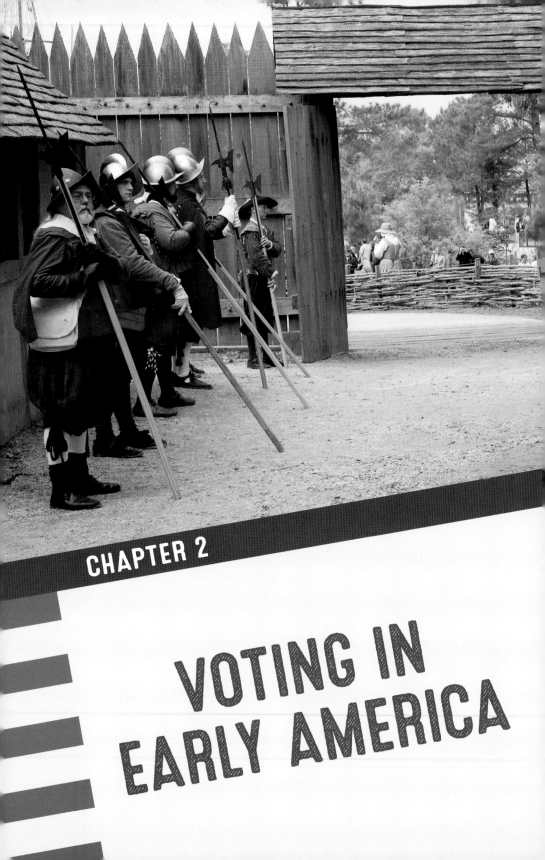

CHAPTER 2

VOTING IN EARLY AMERICA

Today, people can visit James Fort in Jamestown, Virginia, where English settlers first lived.

Before 1965, the United States had routinely denied voting rights to a large portion of its population. The first English settlement, which would eventually become part of the 13 British colonies, was founded at Jamestown in 1607. When the 105 colonists arrived, they carried with them a list of seven potential leaders. This group of seven, all selected in England, was to become the Jamestown council, the governing body of the new colony. From that list of seven council members, a president would be elected. In the final election, six councilmen voted—only 6 percent of the population.[1] These voters selected Edward Maria Wingfield as their first president.

COLONIAL ELECTIONS AND REPRESENTATION

Between the early 1600s and the mid-1700s, many more settlers arrived, and the 13 colonies were established along the Eastern Seaboard. The King of England selected the governor of each colony except Connecticut and Rhode Island. It was common for the governor to select candidates for key government positions, such as sheriffs, justices of the peace, coroners, and clerks.

The King of England selected Massachusetts's governors, including John Leverett, who was governor from 1673 to 1679.

Colonists could vote for those who would represent them in the lower house of government assemblies, the equivalent of the state assemblies today. But the number of colonists who were actually allowed to vote was quite limited. In most colonies, only white men 21 years old or older who owned property and paid taxes could vote. More often than not, the right to vote was denied to Native Americans, women, and those who were enslaved, although free African Americans and women who owned property could vote in some colonies. Sometimes, people of a particular religion were not allowed to vote. In five predominantly Protestant colonies, Catholics could not vote. In another four colonies, people of the Jewish faith could not vote.

DEMOCRACY IS A DIRTY WORD

In the early days of the United States, the government was by no means a democracy. In fact, the Founding Fathers considered a democracy to be a very disorganized system run by those who were not considered educated enough to have a say in government. But what they were criticizing was actually a very specific type of democracy, a direct democracy. In a direct democracy, people participate directly in government decision making, such as passing laws. In reality, the United States is a republic—a form of government in which the people elect representatives to stand up for their interests at government meetings. Another term for *republic* is *representative democracy*.

TAXATION WITHOUT REPRESENTATION

As the colonies became more established, the people living there began to demand a greater stake in government back in their home country. Britain insisted that British representatives in England could adequately represent the interests of the colonists. The colonists disagreed. Then, when Britain began putting taxes on everyday goods such as tea, the colonists protested. They did not think they should have to pay taxes to a government that did not allow them representation. Eventually, the colonists' accusations of taxation without representation became one of the causes of the American Revolutionary War (1775–1783).

When the Founding Fathers signed the Declaration of Independence in 1776, most colonies rewrote their state constitutions to deny women the right to vote.

VOTING AFTER THE REVOLUTION

In the aftermath of the war, some states eliminated requirements that citizens must own land to vote, but the states held on to the rule that voters must pay taxes. By 1790, all states did away with rules banning people of certain religions from voting. During this same time, free African Americans were able to vote in Maryland, Massachusetts, New York, North Carolina, Pennsylvania, and Vermont.

But this slight expansion of voting rights would not be long-lived. By 1807, male legislators officially outlawed women's right to vote in all states. And, after 1819, any

In 1776, women in the state of New Jersey who owned property and paid taxes were allowed to vote.

new state entering the Union denied voting rights to African Americans.

SECOND GREAT AWAKENING

In the 1820s, a religious revival swept through the northern United States. This revival, known as the Second Great Awakening, would shape social reform movements into the next century. Abolitionism—an antislavery movement—and the women's rights movement both began during the Great Awakening.

One of the most important rights enjoyed by white men in the United States but denied to African Americans and women was the right to vote. Abolitionists believed all free people of color should have the right to vote, which would give them the freedom to fully participate in the democratic process. Without that right, African Americans were not equal to their white peers.

The abolitionist movement had gained a large following by the early 1830s. In 1831, William Lloyd Garrison, a white abolitionist in Boston, Massachusetts, had started an abolitionist newspaper called the *Liberator*. In the paper, Garrison published firsthand accounts from slaves who had escaped to freedom in the North. Abolitionist groups such as the American Anti-Slavery Society began to recruit members,

Garrison's newspaper had readers in both the United States and Britain.

FREDERICK DOUGLASS

Former slaves such as Frederick Douglass and Sojourner Truth often spoke at meetings of the Anti-Slavery Society. By telling their stories, they were able to convince those who attended the meetings to join the abolitionist movement. Douglass was born into slavery. He experienced firsthand the brutalities of the practice. In 1838, when he was 20 years old, Douglass escaped to New York City, where he got married and worked on his education. In April 1865, Douglass spoke in Boston at the annual meeting of the Massachusetts Anti-Slavery Society. In his speech "What the Black Man Wants," Douglass talked about the importance of granting African Americans the right to vote. He said, "By depriving us of suffrage, you affirm our incapacity to form an intelligent judgment respecting public men and public measures; you declare before the world that we are unfit to exercise the elective franchise, and by this means lead us to undervalue ourselves, to put a low estimate upon ourselves, and to feel that we have no possibilities like other men."[2]

Douglass wrote three influential autobiographies that helped encourage abolitionists.

hold meetings, and gather supplies such as clothing and food for recently freed slaves. By 1838, the Anti-Slavery Society had 250,000 members.[3]

AFTER THE CIVIL WAR

In 1861, the American Civil War (1861–1865) began. Southern states fought Northern states. One of the biggest issues of the war was slavery. Southern states wanted to keep slavery alive, whereas Northern states fought to end the practice. Abolitionists had a great deal to celebrate in the final days of the Civil War in 1865. On January 31, 1865, Congress passed the Thirteenth Amendment. Ratified on December 6, 1865, it granted African Americans freedom from slavery. Recently

CASTING A BALLOT: HOW PEOPLE VOTED

In colonial America, there were no voting booths, and voters did not have a secret ballot as they do today. Instead, voters would call out the name of the candidate they wished to vote for as they walked into the polling station. Then a voting official would make a mark to indicate that the vote had been cast. It wasn't until the early 1800s that paper ballots were introduced, but even then, the ballots were not private. Voters selected the name of the candidate on a piece of paper. Each candidate was assigned a ballot in a specific color, so it was easy to determine whom a voter selected. By the late 1800s, secret ballots had become commonplace to reduce the risk of bribery and threats.

BLACK CODES

From 1865 to 1866, Southern states passed a number of laws, called black codes, designed to restrict the employment of free African Americans. Mississippi and South Carolina were the first to pass such laws. Mississippi passed a law that required African Americans to have written proof of their employment for the year each January. If a worker left a job before the contract was up, he or she could be forced to pay back wages or face arrest. In South Carolina, a code dictated that African-American laborers could work only as servants or farmers. Those who worked outside those occupations were forced to pay a tax of $10 to $100 per year.[4] Unemployed African Americans were often forced to work at plantations or else pay a fine. In addition, it was against the law for African Americans to marry white people and to own guns. Punishment for committing a crime was often much harsher for African Americans than for white people, and often African Americans were given the death penalty or lynched by white people, who rarely faced punishment for the same crime.

freed slaves signed up with the Union troops, providing the North with a final burst of power needed to defeat the Confederate army.

The celebratory mood would be short-lived. Five days after the South surrendered to the North on April 9, 1865, President Abraham Lincoln was shot by John Wilkes Booth, a Confederate sympathizer, and soon died. The nation was left to piece the North and South together and rebuild the war-torn Southern states under the leadership of former vice president

Andrew Johnson, a Southerner, who was sworn in to take Lincoln's place.

In May 1865, President Johnson proposed a reconstruction act that strongly favored wealthy plantation owners in the South. The act placed much of the power to govern, pass laws, and rebuild in the hands of the states, leaving very little control to the federal government. Southern states quickly took advantage of President Johnson's lenient act and began passing laws that discriminated against African Americans.

But Johnson's reconstruction act wasn't in effect for long. In the 1866 election, voters overwhelmingly elected candidates from Lincoln's antislavery Republican Party. The new legislators overruled President Johnson's policies and passed the First Reconstruction Act in 1867. Johnson vetoed the act, but Congress overrode his veto overwhelmingly to make it law. The act, which divided the South into five military districts, clearly defined how the new Southern governments were to be established.

THE FIFTEENTH AMENDMENT

As part of the Reconstruction Act, the Fifteenth Amendment was ratified in 1870. The amendment prohibited states from denying a male citizen the right to vote based on race, color, or previous condition of servitude.

HARPER'S WEEKLY.
A JOURNAL OF CIVILIZATION.

Vol. XI.—No. 568.] NEW YORK, SATURDAY, NOVEMBER 16, 1867. [SINGLE COPIES TEN CENTS.
[$4.00 PER YEAR IN ADVANCE.

Entered according to Act of Congress, in the Year 1867, by Harper & Brothers, in the Clerk's Office of the District Court for the Southern District of New York.

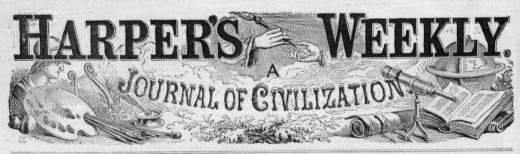

Harper's Weekly magazine shows African Americans voting during the 1867 election.

For the first time in the history of the United States, African Americans in the South made their voices heard through the political process—they exercised their right to vote. With the help of white Republicans in the South, the African-American community voted in Republican representatives throughout the South. This shift in political power had a dramatic effect on the Southern United States.

By the 1880s, African-American men not only voted in elections but were also elected to office. Hiram Rhoades Revels became the first African American elected to the US Congress. A dozen other African-American men won congressional seats during this decade. And more than 600 African Americans were elected to state legislatures and local offices in the South.[5]

DISCUSSION STARTERS

- If you were to make the rules about who could vote in a new country, what would they be and why?

- Do you think the colonists had good reason to protest British taxation of goods? Why or why not?

- Imagine you were in the audience listening to Frederick Douglass tell his story of life as a slave and his escape to freedom. Would his words have convinced you to become an abolitionist? Why or why not?

- What was the purpose of the black codes and why do you think Southern states passed them into law?

CHAPTER 3

WOMEN'S SUFFRAGE

Sisters Angelina, *left*, and Sarah Grimké
supported both the abolitionist and women's
suffrage movements.

Many women played a key role in the passage of the
Fifteenth Amendment. Women such as Angelina Grimké,
Sarah Grimké, Lucretia Mott, and Elizabeth Cady Stanton, all
active abolitionists, rolled up their sleeves and did whatever
they could for the movement. They petitioned Congress,
wrote articles for abolitionist publications, and distributed
flyers announcing antislavery organization meetings. Women
tolerated discrimination against themselves to have a voice
in the movement.

SPEAKING OUT

At a time when it was not socially accepted for women to speak out in public, sisters Angelina Grimké and Sarah Grimké gave speeches about the evils of slavery to mixed audiences of men and women. Clergymen severely criticized the Grimkés for taking a public stance on slavery, but the women were not discouraged. They continued to speak out against the evils of slavery.

Abolitionists Elizabeth Cady Stanton and Lucretia Mott had their own stories of discrimination. When they tried to attend the World Anti-Slavery Convention in London in 1840, they were denied seats on the convention floor simply because they were women. These blatant acts of discrimination inspired Stanton, Mott, and the Grimké sisters to take the first steps in the fight for women's rights, including a woman's right to vote.

WOMEN'S RIGHTS CONVENTION

The discrimination they faced at the Anti-Slavery Convention didn't discourage Stanton and Mott. Instead, it made them realize that it was time to take a stand for their own rights as well. So in 1848, Stanton and Mott organized the first Women's Rights Convention at Wesleyan Chapel in Seneca Falls, New York. The gathering, which was held on July 19 and 20, drew an audience of more than 200 people, including 40 men.[1] Just as women supported the abolitionist movement, many abolitionists also supported the women's rights movement. Formerly enslaved abolitionist Frederick Douglass attended the convention in Seneca Falls and signed the Declaration of Sentiments.

On the first day, which was for women only, Stanton and Mott drafted a Declaration of Sentiments and Grievances. The declaration, which was modeled after the Declaration of Independence, stated, "We hold these truths to be self-evident: that all men and women are created equal; that they are endowed by their creator with certain inalienable rights."[2]

On the second day, anyone was invited to attend. Twelve resolutions were passed, declaring that women be granted certain rights, including the right to an equal education and the right to equal treatment under the law. It was the ninth resolution that brought controversy to the convention. It stated, "Resolved, that it is the

Stanton speaks at the Women's Rights Convention.

THE CIVIL WAR PUTS EFFORTS ON HOLD

In the decade after the Women's Rights Convention at Seneca Falls, the United States was looking more like a divided nation than a united one. Legislators from the proslavery Southern states defended their plantation-driven, slave-dependent economy, while those in the North became increasingly opposed to slavery. Many of the women who had gone to Seneca Falls now focused their attention on what they could do to help the abolitionist movement. Even those who organized the first Women's Rights Convention, including Stanton, put the issue of women's rights and the fight for women's suffrage on hold until after the Civil War.

duty of the women of this country to secure to themselves their sacred right to the elective franchise."[3]

The resolution, which called for women to be granted the right to vote, was presented by Stanton. Mott was against including women's suffrage in the resolutions, simply because she thought it was asking too much and would detract from the movement. After a heated debate, the resolution was approved by the convention, but not without objection. Some previous women's rights supporters chose to leave the movement because of the ninth resolution.

Although the meeting at Seneca Falls was not taken seriously by opponents of women's rights, the convention did mark the beginning of the women's suffrage movement. Two weeks later, a second meeting of women called in Rochester,

New York, drew an even larger audience. From that point forward, women's rights conventions were held every year.

ONE MISSION, TWO SCHOOLS OF THOUGHT

In Seneca Falls, the women in attendance agreed on the need to stand up for women's rights. But they didn't always agree on how to go about it. Two distinct groups emerged from the Seneca Falls meeting, each with very different approaches to the Fifteenth Amendment, which granted African Americans the right to vote.

The National Woman Suffrage Association (NWSA), founded in 1869 by Stanton and Susan B. Anthony, dedicated its time and efforts to changing federal laws that denied women the right to vote. NWSA decided not to support the Fifteenth Amendment because it didn't grant suffrage to women.

The American Women's Suffrage Association (AWSA), on the other hand, fully supported the Fifteenth Amendment and actively campaigned to pass it. The AWSA was led by Henry Blackwell, Julia Ward Howe, and Lucy Stone, a dedicated abolitionist and women's rights advocate who believed in equal rights for all. Unlike the NWSA, which worked on many fronts to improve rights for women across the board, the AWSA focused on women's suffrage. The AWSA also took a different strategy

WINNING THE VOTE STATE BY STATE

The AWSA's efforts to win women's voting rights by focusing on passing legislation at the state level produced results. Wyoming Territory was the first to grant women the right to vote, in 1869. In the 1890s, nearly 20 years before a federal law granting women the right to vote would pass, women in the states of Colorado, Utah, and Idaho were voting in at least some elections. Each of these western states added an amendment to its constitution that granted women the right to vote. Between 1910 and 1918, several more states and a US territory passed women's suffrage laws. These included the Alaska Territory, Arizona, Arkansas, California, Illinois, Indiana, Kansas, Michigan, Montana, Nebraska, Nevada, New York, North Dakota, Oklahoma, Oregon, South Dakota, and Washington. In 1916, Jeannette Rankin became the first woman elected to Congress. She represented the state of Montana.

than the NWSA, putting effort into changing voting laws at the state level. But in part due to this split in the women's rights movement, women's suffrage efforts lost momentum.

A UNITED FRONT

In 1890, however, under the leadership of Stanton, the NWSA and the AWSA merged to form the National American Woman Suffrage Association (NAWSA). The two groups set aside their differences and came up with a new strategy. All along, the women's rights movement had claimed that women should have the right to vote because they are men's equals. Now the NAWSA proclaimed they should be able to vote because they were different from men.

This approach pleased political groups of all stripes who were willing to back the NAWSA's new approach. Temperance groups, which were Christian women's organizations that fought to outlaw alcohol production and consumption, liked the idea of women's suffrage because women were more likely to support temperance efforts. Middle-class white voters were for a woman's right to vote

WOMAN'S CHRISTIAN TEMPERANCE UNION

Against the backdrop of a deep economic depression, women in Cleveland, Ohio, banded together to form the Woman's Christian Temperance Union (WCTU) in 1874. Although the organization's original purpose was to shut down the sale of alcohol in local saloons, the WCTU eventually broadened its scope. In what was called a "Do Everything" campaign, WCTU president Frances Willard encouraged women to get involved at the local level in all areas of social reform, including prison reforms, public health, and working conditions. In 1881, the WCTU began to work toward women's suffrage. The WCTU was the largest women's organization in the country during the 1800s, influencing and spinning off several other social reform movements. One of these, the National Association of Colored Women, was founded by Frances Ellen Watkins Harper in 1896. Watkins Harper was known for the work she did to improve the lives of African Americans as head of the WCTU's Department for Work among Negros.

because they wanted to increase the number of white voters at the polls.

DRASTIC MEASURES

By the 1910s, some women had grown tired of the slow pace of reform. One of the most confrontational women's rights activists was Alice Paul. Paul had spent time in England, where suffragists took to the streets to march, preach, and picket in the name of women's rights. Realizing these more militant tactics could be effective in the United States, Paul joined the NAWSA and began staging demonstrations.

Paul saw an opportunity to garner some attention for the cause on March 3, 1913, the day before Woodrow Wilson was inaugurated, by staging a parade in the name of women's suffrage. With more than 5,000 participants from every state in the Union, the parade attracted the attention of hundreds of thousands of spectators.[4]

In January 1917, more activists took radical approaches. They had decided that lobbying the legislature and leading women's vote campaigns on a state-by-state basis were not getting the attention of the American people and the press. So they staged hunger strikes and organized crowds of people to form picket lines at the White House. All of these efforts were strategically orchestrated to publicize their cause.

Paul stands in front of a suffrage flag in 1920. Its colors were purple, white, and gold.

To push President Wilson to pass a law legalizing women's suffrage, Paul organized a protest called Silent Sentinels, in which women held signs and picketed in front of the White House. The signs read, "Mr. President, what will you do for woman suffrage?"[5] The protesters were arrested, and some, including Paul, were sent to prison. In retaliation, Paul staged a hunger strike. She was force-fed with feeding tubes and told that if she didn't eat she would be committed to a mental hospital. Yet Paul held her ground.

CARRIE CHAPMAN CATT

Although Paul brought the issue of women's suffrage into the public spotlight with dramatic protests and hunger strikes, it was Catt's lighter touch that would ultimately convince President Wilson to endorse a plan for women's suffrage. Catt, who was twice president of the NAWSA and founder of the League of Women Voters in 1920, worked behind the scenes to diplomatically convince President Wilson of the importance of women's suffrage. Along with a plan to campaign for suffrage through state and federal channels, Catt expressed a willingness to compromise, accepting partial suffrage in resistant states. She argued, "Everybody counts in applying democracy. And there will never be a true democracy until every responsible and law-abiding adult in it, without regard to race, sex, color or creed has his or her own inalienable and unpurchasable voice in government."[6] Through organization of an army of volunteers, targeted speeches, and thoughtful campaigns, Catt was able to win a victory for women's suffrage with the passing of the Nineteenth Amendment In 1920. At the heart of her effective campaign was Catt's ardent belief that women should have control over their own lives and those of their children. Without the right to vote, Catt argued, women's sense of self-worth suffered. With the right to vote, women would be an asset to democracy, helping to improve life for everyone. With a voice in the political process, women would be a force for peace in the world.

Catt's influential speeches and ability to run organizations made her a prominent leader in the women's suffrage movement.

Wilson despised Paul's tactics. But he finally relented to the women's suffrage movement. In a 1918 letter to NAWSA president Carrie Chapman Catt, Wilson wrote, "I agree without reservation that the full and sincere democratic reconstruction of the world for which we are striving, and which we are determined to bring about at any cost, will not have been completely or adequately attained until women are admitted to the suffrage."[7] Paul survived, was released, and went on to campaign for the Equal Rights Amendment and to be a voice for other women's issues.

WORLD WAR I

In 1917, as Paul and the other suffragists stepped up their protest tactics, the United States entered World War I (1914–1918). Women throughout the nation banded together to do what they could to support the war. They sold war bonds, knitted for the troops, conserved food, and sent care packages and relief supplies overseas. Many of these efforts were coordinated by social reform organizations that had been active before the war, including the suffrage movement.

Women also took a more active role in the American workforce during the war, filling in for men who had left for the front lines. Women not only took jobs in factories but also served as nurses, joined the navy, and signed up for the marine

Women weigh wire coils at a factory during World War I.

corps. Earning their own paychecks and making valuable contributions to the American economy and war effort fueled a sense of empowerment among women.

This experience served to reinforce the argument that women should be granted the right to vote as well. Suffragists argued that a nation willing to send soldiers overseas to fight for democracy in other countries should allow women to fully participate in democracy at home. World War I gave the suffrage movement the momentum it needed to finally push through legislation guaranteeing women the right to vote.

THE NINETEENTH AMENDMENT

On August 18, 1920, the Nineteenth Amendment to the constitution was ratified at last, granting women the right to vote. Seventy-two years after Stanton announced in Seneca Falls that women would fight for the right to vote, her dream had become a reality. On November 2, 1920, women throughout the nation went to the polls for the first time. More than eight million women cast ballots in the election.[8] Although women's suffrage certainly increased the number of voting Americans, it did not make a noticeable change in the end results. Women tended to vote in the same way their husbands or fathers did. But the battle was not over yet. In the South, where a majority of legislators were strongly opposed to granting women the right to vote, African-American women were turned away at the polls.

DISCUSSION STARTERS

- Why do you think so many abolitionists also supported women's rights? What are the similarities and differences between the missions of the two movements?

- How did the temperance movement empower women in the 1800s?

- If you were a suffragist in the late 1800s, would you have been more like Paul or Catt? Why?

CHAPTER 4

CIVIL RIGHTS MOVEMENT

A cartoon depicts members of the White League, an organization that tried to keep African Americans from voting, discriminating against African-American voters.

Even though the women's suffrage movement had achieved a giant feat with the passing of the Nineteenth Amendment, disenfranchisement among African Americans was widespread, especially in the South. In fact, as soon as the Fifteenth Amendment was ratified in 1870, states opposed to African-American suffrage took measures at polling booths to deny African Americans the right to vote.

Through literacy tests and grandfather clauses, these US citizens were routinely denied the right to vote. Many African Americans had been denied access to a formal education, so they could not read and therefore could not pass a literacy test. Yet grandfather clauses stated that illiterate white people whose ancestors had been able to vote in the 1860s could skip literacy tests. A grandfather clause directly targeted African Americans, most of whom were descended from slaves, who did not have their freedom nor the right to vote in the 1860s.

BEHIND THE SCENES

The dread of being forced to take a literacy test or be otherwise turned away from polling stations prevented most African Americans from even attempting to vote. But intimidation was at play as well.

During the Reconstruction Era, when white Southerners believed that their old way of life was in danger of disappearing for good, white supremacist organizations spread throughout the South. Often under cover of darkness, members of groups such as the KKK used violence and threats to make sure African Americans stayed away from the polls. KKK members physically assaulted or even lynched African Americans during the height of KKK activity from the 1860s to the 1870s.

The KKK also threatened local Republican leaders of all backgrounds, as well as African Americans who dared to stand up to white authority. In addition, African Americans were warned that if they attempted to vote they would be fired from their jobs. At a time when a deep economic depression had settled over the South, no one could afford to lose a job. Voting simply wasn't worth the risk.

THE SOUTH RETURNS TO THE DEMOCRATIC PARTY

After the election of Rutherford B. Hayes in 1876, Southern states came under the control of the Democratic Party. At the time, the Democratic Party mainly consisted of conservative politicians who had been in favor of slavery before the war. In the postwar Reconstruction Era, Southern Democrats resented being forced to grant equal rights to African Americans.

With Democrats in power in the South, those who still believed African Americans should not be granted the same rights as white people were

The KKK's disguises were intended to keep people from recognizing the members and also to inspire fear.

POLITICAL POWER IN THE SOUTH

In the closely contested presidential race of 1876, Republican candidate Rutherford B. Hayes needed the backing of Florida, Louisiana, and South Carolina to win. So Hayes met with moderate Southern Democrats who demanded that he pull Northern militia out of the South. In what was called the Compromise of 1877, Hayes agreed to withdraw the troops. He also promised to allow the Democratic Party to have control over the South. In return, the South would certify his presidency. The compromise officially ended the Reconstruction Era—and handed political power in the South to the white minority.

elected to all levels of office. Some elected officials even had ties to the KKK or other white supremacist organizations. Under the authority of these legislators, discrimination remained ingrained in the South. Politicians continued to pass laws that denied African Americans basic rights, including the right to vote, at the state and local levels.

FIGHTING FOR EQUAL OPPORTUNITY

Racism, discrimination, and violence against African Americans were certainly not limited to the South. Race-related riots and African-American lynchings in Springfield, Illinois, pushed one outraged group of citizens to take action. In August 1908, rumors of two accounts in which African-American men had assaulted white women caused an angry mob of white people

IDA B. WELLS

Ida B. Wells was a fierce advocate for African-American rights. In 1884, Wells bought a first-class ticket on a Memphis, Tennessee, train, but because she was African American, the conductor tried to force her to move. Wells bit the conductor's hand and he promptly threw her off the train. Wells sued, winning the case in the lower courts but losing in the appeal. Wells said, "I have firmly believed all along that the law was on our side and would, when we appealed to it, give us justice. I feel shorn of that belief and utterly discouraged."[1] She became the co-owner and editor of the *Free Speech and Headlight*, an African-American newspaper based in Memphis. Using the pen name Iola, Wells spoke out against lynching and voter disenfranchisement and encouraged African Americans to stand up for themselves. In 1892, her friend Tom Moss was lynched with a couple of other African Americans for defending Moss's store from a white mob. Wells lashed out through articles in her newspaper. Wells left Memphis in protest, taking refuge in England, where she spoke about the evils of lynching in America. On her return to the United States, Wells stayed away from Memphis for fear she might be killed by angry white people. She moved to the Chicago, Illinois, area, where she married Ferdinand Barnett, a lawyer. In 1896, Wells became a founding member of the National Association of Colored Women. In 1909, she helped found the National Association for the Advancement of Colored People. She fought to end the practice of lynching for the remainder of her days.

Wells was called a crusader for justice.

to riot in the streets. They gathered at the county courthouse and demanded that the suspects be released to them for lynching. When the sheriff told them the men had been moved to another area for protection, the mob roamed the streets in search of other African Americans to lynch. They found and promptly lynched barbershop owner Scott Burton and 84-year-old William Donegan. That day, several locally owned businesses and homes were destroyed, and six African Americans were shot.[2]

Horrified by the Springfield riot and the continued practice of lynching, a group of 60 white and African-American civil rights activists, including Jane Addams, Ida B. Wells-Barnett, and W. E. B. DuBois, met in Springfield to discuss what could be done. They formed the National Association for the Advancement of Colored People (NAACP) in 1909, an organization that would advocate for civil rights, fight for equal opportunity under the law, and work to register African Americans to vote.

Early on, the NAACP became a voice for disenfranchised African Americans in the courtroom. In *Guinn v. United States* in 1910, one of many examples, the NAACP won a key victory against an Oklahoma grandfather clause that discriminated against voters. The organization also spent 30 years pushing to pass anti-lynching legislation by supporting the Dyer Bill, but it never passed in the Senate.

CONTINUED DISCRIMINATION AT THE POLLS

Despite the efforts of the NAACP, little had changed for African-American voters by the 1950s. Several Southern

An election official tells two African-American voters they cannot vote in the white primary. Some cities in the 1940s allowed African Americans to vote only in the general elections.

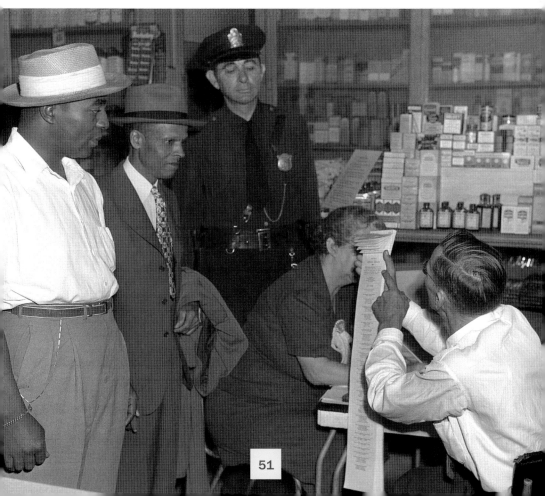

states continued to enforce laws similar to those in effect in the post-Reconstruction Era. Literacy tests were still required. In Alabama, Arkansas, Mississippi, Texas, and Virginia, African-American voters had to pay a poll tax. And in Alabama, voters had to complete a written test on the Constitution and government to be able to vote. But these tests were often confusingly worded, intended to make the voters fail. In truth, many of the white voters in Alabama were not capable of passing such a test, yet they were allowed to vote.

CIVIL RIGHTS ACT OF 1957

The NAACP put pressure on the federal government to pass civil rights legislation that would enforce African-American voting rights. After a drawn-out battle to gather enough votes in the Congress and Senate, President Dwight D. Eisenhower signed the Civil Rights Act into law on September 9, 1957.

The act was the first piece of civil rights legislation to pass since Reconstruction in the 1870s. Although the bill was significantly watered down by Southern Democrats, who did not like provisions that allowed the Justice Department to send troops to enforce civil rights laws, it still took important steps to protect African-American voting rights. The Civil Rights Act also added a Civil Rights Division within the Justice Department and established the US Civil Rights Commission, which looked into voting rights violation claims.

A FOCUS ON SELMA

Despite the federal government's new commitment to protect the civil rights of African Americans, discrimination continued on a local level in many Southern states. Perhaps the most grievous offender was the state of Alabama, where local law enforcement systematically and blatantly disregarded federal laws designed to guarantee voting rights to African Americans. At Alabama polling

VOTING DISCRIMINATION

Fanny Lou Hamer worked on a cotton plantation in the Mississippi River Delta. Hamer was one of 18 African Americans who boarded a bus to Indianola, Mississippi, on August 31, 1962, with the intent of registering to vote.[3] When they arrived in Indianola, only Hamer and one man in the group were allowed to fill out an application, but both failed the literacy test. All 18 got back on the bus and headed home to Ruleville, Mississippi. But along the way, police pulled over the bus and arrested the driver on charges that the bus was too yellow. Hamer and the other riders pooled what money they had to pay the fine, and the bus driver was allowed to continue on. When Hamer finally returned to her home on the plantation, the plantation owner, W. D. Marlow, had already learned about her attempts to register. When Hamer would not withdraw her application to vote, Marlow kicked her off the plantation. From that point forward, Hamer dedicated her life to civil rights action, helping register African Americans to vote, working toward desegregation, and doing relief work for the poor in the Mississippi Delta.

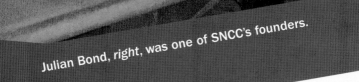

Julian Bond, right, was one of SNCC's founders.

stations, registrars continued to require that African Americans pass a literacy test and a test on the finer points of the US Constitution before they could cast a ballot.

Civil rights groups began focusing their efforts where they were needed most. In 1963, SNCC headed to Selma, Dallas County, Alabama. Selma, where the population was 57 percent African American, had only 1 percent of African Americans on the voting rolls.[4] Here, SNCC would begin a campaign to help African Americans register to vote.

SNCC worked with the Dallas County Voters League (DCVL), a voting rights group based in Selma. Through grassroots organizing, SNCC and the DCVL organized a Citizenship School to help prepare African Americans for the literacy tests

DALLAS COUNTY VOTERS LEAGUE

In the 1930s, Amelia Boynton Robinson was one of the few African Americans in Dallas County who could vote. To make it possible for more African Americans to vote, Robinson, her husband, and a few others decided to form the DCVL. The DCVL held meetings in churches and in peoples' homes where they would teach African Americans how to take the literacy tests. When Robinson's husband began to escort groups of three or four people to register in Selma, he was told he was bringing too many at once. So Robinson invited King to come to Selma in 1965 to help register voters.

they needed to pass to vote. Other SNCC members went door-to-door to encourage African Americans to vote.

Yet after three years of these efforts, the activists grew discouraged. It remained nearly impossible for African Americans to register to vote. Even those who could pass the literacy test were rejected. African Americans were fired from their jobs for trying to register. White employers who let their employees register also faced consequences. Some African Americans were beaten or arrested for attempting to register. All the while, federal, state, and local governments did nothing to enforce the Civil Rights Act.

FREEDOM SUMMER

In the summer of 1964, SNCC and another civil rights group, the Congress of Racial Equality (CORE), joined forces to coordinate a voter drive in Mississippi. More than 1,000 mostly white volunteers and activists came from around the country to help.[5] But their efforts were met with violence and harassment. A campaign of violence coordinated by the KKK, police, and state officials was designed to intimidate volunteers and suppress the voter registration efforts. During the Freedom Summer, activists lived in constant fear of arson, beatings, and arrests as they worked to register voters. At least three activists were murdered in the beginning of that Mississippi summer, including CORE workers Michael Schwerner and James Chaney, as well as Andrew Goodman, a student from New York.

STEPPING UP EFFORTS

In early 1965, civil rights activists decided it

was time to shine a spotlight on Selma. Activists from around the country descended on the town to take a stand for voting rights. King and the SCLC had been invited to Selma to help SNCC step up voter registration for African Americans. During a two-month period, King walked hundreds of African Americans to register to vote. Nearly 2,000 demonstrators were arrested by Sheriff James Clark for delinquency, contempt of court, and marching without a permit.[6] But not one name was added to the voting rolls.

All was not lost, however. Voter registration efforts in Selma would eventually lead to the march to Montgomery on March 7, 1965. The violent crackdown by Selma police outraged the nation and ultimately pushed President Johnson to ask Congress to pass the Voting Rights Act.

DISCUSSION STARTERS

- How did the KKK keep African Americans away from voting stations? Why do you think the KKK didn't want African Americans to vote?

- Why do you think states passed laws that denied African Americans the right to vote, even though the Fifteenth Amendment had been passed?

- Do you think it was fair for civil rights activists to focus national attention on Selma when voting rights were being denied in many other parts of the country as well? Why or why not?

CHAPTER 5

UPHOLDING THE VOTING RIGHTS ACT

Hundreds of voters registered to vote on August 9, 1965, in Americus, Georgia, after the Voting Rights Act was signed.

Under the Voting Rights Act of 1965, voter registration in the states of Alabama, Alaska, Arizona, Georgia, Louisiana, Mississippi, South Carolina, Texas, and Virginia—plus counties and municipalities such as Brooklyn, Manhattan, and the Bronx in New York—all fell under observation by the federal government. These states, counties, and municipalities had a track record of requiring African Americans to pass literacy tests or recite the Constitution to earn the right to vote. In some of these targeted areas, African Americans made up more than half the population.

DOING THE WORK

In places like Selma, the Voting Rights Act proved to be effective. In the early 1960s, only 1 percent of African Americans in Selma were registered to vote, although African Americans made up more than one-half of the town's population.[1] By 1970, 66 percent of African Americans across the South were registered to vote.[2] Today, African Americans vote in Selma and are elected to office. In 2016, Selma elected Darrio Melton, an African-American mayor; Terri Sewell, an African-American congresswoman; and five African-American council members.[3]

Yet only a small percentage of them were registered to vote. The purpose of the Voting Rights Act was to ensure that voting rolls in these states accurately reflected their populations.

SECTION 5

Section 5 of the Voting Rights Act has been called the heart and soul of this important piece of civil rights legislation. Section 5 states that in jurisdictions that had been singled out in Section 4 of the Voting Rights Act—mainly voting districts in the South known for discrimination—the states could not make changes to voting laws until the US attorney general or a US district court could verify that the change did not result in discrimination.

The importance of Section 5 has been acknowledged across party lines many times in the years since 1965. Whenever the section came up for review, it was extended with the overwhelming support of Congress. Four Republican presidents signed Section 5 legislation, extending it by five years in 1970, by seven years in 1975, by 25 years in 1982, and by another 25 years in 2006.[4]

AN AFRICAN-AMERICAN PRESIDENT

The historic election of Barack Obama, an African-American senator from the state of Illinois, to the presidency in 2008 demonstrated the power of the Voting Rights Act. In the election, voter turnout was the highest it had been in more than 40 years. But it was the makeup of the voting population that swept Obama into office.

In 2008, two million more African Americans, 600,000 more Asians, and two million more Latinos went to the polls than in 2004.[5] In Maryland, Mississippi, Nevada, Ohio, and South Carolina, more than 70 percent of voters cast ballots.[6] These results would not have been possible without the Voting Rights Act in place.

PREJUDICE SURFACES

Although the election of the first African-American president drew a more diverse electorate to the polls, it also brought racism and prejudice bubbling to the surface. In formerly Confederate states, votes for Obama among white voters lagged behind those in other areas of the country by 3 to 5 percentage points.[7] And, in a study by Seth Stephens-Davidowitz, Google searches for demeaning jokes about African Americans spiked in states where Obama did not do well in the 2008 election.

OVERTURNING SECTION 4

In December 2012, Shelby County, Alabama, along with five states, petitioned the Supreme Court, asking that it overrule the Section 5 provision of the Voting Rights Act. Shelby County claimed the provision was no longer needed. The racial discrimination that blocked African-American efforts to vote in Southern states during the civil rights era wasn't an issue anymore. Section 5, the plaintiffs claimed, had become outdated.

The Supreme Court debated the contemporary relevance of Section 5. More than once, Chief Justice John Roberts asked the parties defending the Voting Rights Act why all states are not covered under Section 5 if voter suppression happens in other states as well. "Things have changed in the South," Justice Roberts said.[8] Solicitor General Donald Verrilli, representing the Obama administration, countered that there were real reasons to treat states differently.

But in the end, the Supreme Court decided otherwise. On June 25, 2013, in a 5–4 vote, the court overturned Section 4 of the Voting Rights Act.[9] This was the section that named which states and jurisdictions needed federal approval to adjust voting laws and districts. Without it, Section 5 cannot function.

PERSPECTIVES
JOHN LEWIS

As Georgia representative John Lewis sat in on the Supreme Court deliberations over Section 5, he could not believe what he was hearing. The justices referred to Section 5 as an outdated piece of legislation that infringed on state sovereignty. The states called out in Section 5 should not be treated differently from other states, the justices argued. Times had changed. But what brought Lewis nearly to tears was Justice Antonin Scalia's use of the term "perpetuation of racial entitlement."[10]

For Lewis, the chairman of SNCC who was badly beaten on the Edmund Pettus Bridge during Bloody Sunday in 1965, the right to vote was certainly not a racial entitlement. For him and the many others of the civil rights movement who had nearly given their lives fighting for the right to vote, it was and still is a hard-earned right that still requires protection. To hear the justices talk about how the preclearance protections provided by Section 5 of the Voting Rights Act were no longer needed was beyond shocking. "The right to vote is a racial entitlement?" Lewis asked. "So what happened to the Fourteenth and Fifteenth Amendments? And what happened to the whole struggle to make it possible in the twentieth century, and now in the twenty-first century, for every person to cast a ballot?"[11]

In Congress, Lewis has continued his fight to protect Americans' rights.

Justice Roberts explained that Section 4 was overturned because it pulled from decades-old information that could no longer be true. He said, "Our decision in no way affects the permanent, nationwide ban on racial discrimination in voting found in [Section] 2. . . . Congress may draft another formula based on current conditions."[12] The court said that Section 2 could replace Section 5. Section 2 is a nationwide provision that never expires. It allows plaintiffs to bring forth lawsuits when they believe voting laws discriminate against voters. The disadvantage of relying on Section 2, however, is in the delay

Many elected officials were disappointed in the Supreme Court's ruling on Section 5. Ernest Montgomery, a city council member in Calera, Alabama, believed the Voting Rights Act allowed him to be elected.

of when action can be taken. Section 5 allows the federal government to review proposed laws before they can be passed into law. Under Section 2, on the other hand, laws have taken effect and may be in place for a while before a plaintiff gathers enough evidence to prove civil rights have been violated. In the meantime, civil rights are not protected.

Julie Fernandes, who was deputy assistant attorney general for civil rights under the Obama administration, made the following prediction before the court overturned Section 4: "In a world without Section 5, it would be very difficult for the Justice Department or private plaintiffs, of which there are very few, to identify the places where discrimination is happening and to be responsive enough to stop it from happening before it has a devastating effect."[13]

DISCUSSION STARTERS

- What was the purpose of the Voting Rights Act?
- What evidence is there that proves the Voting Rights Act has been effective?
- Why do you think voter turnout was so high in 2008 when Obama ran for president?
- Do you think Section 4 of the Voting Rights Act should have been overturned? Why or why not?

CHAPTER 6

VOTER ID LAWS

In Texas, election officials must check voters' IDs before allowing them to vote.

Even before Section 4 was overruled in 2013, states were beginning to pass voter ID laws. Voter ID laws require that voters present an approved, government-issued form of ID when they go to vote. Accepted forms of ID vary from state to state, but they usually include valid driver's licenses, state-issued ID cards, or military ID cards. Some states require an ID that has a photo and a signature, whereas others are more lenient.

What happens when a voter shows up at the polls without proper ID varies by state as well. In some states, a voter can cast a provisional ballot and return later with proper ID to have the vote counted officially. In other states, a person without proper ID may still cast an official ballot.

NONCITIZENS CASTING BALLOTS

Concerns about noncitizens casting ballots have been widespread since Obama won the presidential election in 2008. In a survey by YouGov in 2008, 15 percent of noncitizens said they were registered to vote, and 8 percent said they actually voted in the 2008 election.[1] If it is against the law for noncitizens to vote, how is this possible? Those who have a valid driver's license may be allowed to vote at the polls, and, through motor voter laws, may be able to register to vote when they go to renew their driver's license. Debates about what to do about noncitizens who vote are largely divided along partisan lines. Republicans want to crack down on noncitizen voter fraud, claiming that the noncitizen votes cancel out ballots cast by American citizens. Democrats, on the other hand, don't think any action is needed. They argue that claims that noncitizen voting is rampant are difficult to prove. In addition, noncitizens tend to vote for Democratic candidates, making Democrats less inclined to worry.

PREVENTING VOTER FRAUD

To many, this seems like a logical requirement. It makes sense that the officials at polling centers verify that voters are who they say they are. Requiring that voters show a valid ID is one way of ensuring that voters are US citizens who are eligible to vote and they cast only one ballot in their name. Supporters claim that if voters are required to show ID, there will be fewer instances of voter fraud.

Voter fraud is rare. In the 2016 election, investigators were able to find only four documented instances of voter fraud. But fraud has happened. In Chicago, it was discovered that 119 dead people were on the voting rolls, and those 119 have voted 229 times from 2006 to 2016.[2] In 2016, Colorado election officials investigated claims of four instances in which dead voters' names were used to cast ballots.[3] How does this happen? In some cases, instances of voting fraud are accidental. For example, someone may be marked as a deceased relative with the same name. Or they may be true cases of voter fraud. It's not uncommon for states to fail to delete the names of dead voters from the voting rolls. All it takes, then, is for someone with access to those rolls to provide names to potential voters. A voter who strongly favors a particular candidate can then cast a vote in his or her home district and also mail in a ballot to another district to vote in the name of the deceased person.

THE RISK OF DISENFRANCHISEMENT

Those who are opposed to voter ID laws claim that they disproportionately affect minorities, the young, and older adults—groups that tend to vote for Democratic candidates.

Virginia requires voters to show a photo ID. This could be a driver's license, a US passport, a student ID card, or a tribal ID card.

For people in these groups, who are less likely to have standard forms of ID such as driver's licenses or state IDs, the cost and hassle of obtaining the proper ID can prevent them from voting.

Even in states such as Texas, where voters are provided with access to free voting IDs, obtaining these IDs is not really free. An original birth certificate is usually required. Many people don't have original copies of their birth certificates, so they must travel to a county courthouse and pay to get a certified copy. Lack of a car,

DENIED THE RIGHT TO VOTE

Gladys Harris, a 66-year-old African American who lives in Milwaukee, Wisconsin, was one of those who tried to vote in the 2016 election but was unable to. It wasn't easy for Harris to make it to the polling station. She doesn't have a car, so she relies on public transportation. She also has chronic lung disease and a torn ligament in her knee, which makes it difficult to get around. Yet when she arrived at the polling station, she was told that none of the forms of ID she had with her would work to vote. Harris had lost her driver's license just that week, and the registrar denied the use of her Social Security card, Medicare cards, and county bus pass, which included her photo. She was allowed to cast a provisional ballot, but she was unable to make it back to the polling station with proper ID to cast an official ballot in the next few days. Harris's vote, along with those of 300,000 other voters in Wisconsin who went to the polls but lacked proper ID, would not be cast or counted.[4]

other resources, or a friend or relative to help them through the process make it more unlikely that minorities, the young, or older adults will vote.

IT'S POLITICS

Overwhelmingly, the states that have passed strict voter ID laws are those that have a Republican majority. The first two states to require voters to show some form of ID to vote were Arizona and Ohio in 2006. In 2008, Georgia and Indiana followed suit, but these states passed stricter voter ID laws, requiring a photo ID.

The landslide results of midterm elections in 2010 tipped scales in the US House and Senate in favor of the Republican Party. Many of these victories were made possible through the work of the American Legislative Exchange Council

VOTER ID LAWS: AFFECTING MINORITIES

Although voter ID laws are relatively new, studies show that they affect voter turnout. In states with strict voter ID laws—meaning laws that require a valid photo ID in order to cast a ballot—voter turnout among white people remains similar. But in those same states, voter turnout among minority groups, including Latinos, African Americans, and Asians, is negatively affected. In a general election, for example, the gap between the number of white versus Latino voters in strict voter ID states is 13.2 percentage points, whereas the gap in states without strict voter ID laws is 4.9 points.[5]

STATES WITH VOTER ID LAWS

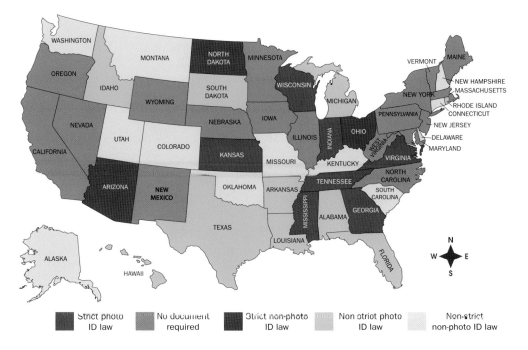

| Strict photo ID law | No document required | Strict non-photo ID law | Non strict photo ID law | Non-strict non-photo ID law |

(ALEC), a conservative organization led by writer Paul Weyrich. ALEC made it a top priority to pass voter ID laws, citing the need to crack down on voter fraud.

STATES PASS VOTER ID LAWS

Weyrich's plan worked. One by one, states with Republican-led governments passed their own voter ID laws. Republican governor Scott Walker signed a voter ID law in the state of Wisconsin in 2011. The law required all voters to present a government-issued photo ID such as a driver's license, military ID, US passport, or signed and dated student ID from an accredited university or college.

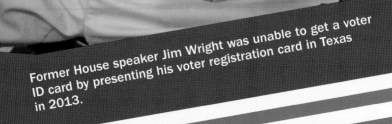

Former House speaker Jim Wright was unable to get a voter ID card by presenting his voter registration card in Texas in 2013.

On November 5, 2013, Texas passed a strict voter ID law, a law the state had tried to pass once before. The first time Texas drafted the law, it was blocked by the federal government under Section 5 of the Voting Rights Act. The federal government had deemed the voter ID law discriminatory. But when Section 4 of the Voting Rights Act was overturned, Texas was able to pass this voter ID law.

As of 2017, 32 states had passed voter ID laws.[6] In many of those states, the laws require that voters present a photo ID to vote. In the first half of 2017 alone, 87 bills to limit access to voting were introduced in 29 states, and strict voter ID laws passed in Arkansas and Iowa.[7] But some states with non-strict voter ID laws are trying to make voting fair. Voters without IDs can give their signatures, which are compared with their registration signatures, to prove they are registered to vote.

DISCUSSION STARTERS

- Do you think voter ID laws prevent voter fraud?

- Can you think of any ways that voter ID laws could be prevented from discriminating against minorities, the young, and older adults?

- Are you for or against voter ID laws? Why or why not?

CHAPTER 7

GERRYMANDERING

Gerrymandering, the intentional redistricting of a state's congressional districts to favor the political party in control, has been a strategy increasingly used by both political parties. Although gerrymandering has been around throughout the history of the United States, the battle over control of districts has heated up in the past ten to fifteen years. Four of the five most partisan state legislature maps, for example, were drawn after 2010, during the Republican response to the election of President Obama. With the Republican Party controlling 33 state legislatures, members

Citizens and members of Congress alike can play the ReDistricting Game, which teaches players how redistricting works.

were in a position to redistrict 204 or more congressional districts, which accounted for almost one-half of the representatives in the House.[1]

HOW GERRYMANDERING WORKS

Every ten years, after census data have been collected, states evaluate districts to make sure they are evenly populated. If they are not, district lines have to be redrawn to adjust for population shifts and create even districts. This is called redistricting, and it's a standard part of the US political system. But redistricting crosses the line into gerrymandering when the political party that holds the majority in the state legislature deliberately creates districts to gain an advantage for itself.

For example, a state may have a population of 100 people, and 60 of those people vote for the yellow party, whereas 40 people vote for the green party. Say the voters are evenly divided in a grid, with those who vote yellow living on one side of the state and the green voters living on the other. The state must be divided into five

GERRY AND SALAMANDER

The concept of redistricting is not new. In fact, the term *gerrymandering* was first coined in 1812, when Governor Elbridge Gerry of Massachusetts redrew districts to improve his likelihood of being elected. Opponents claimed that one of the districts looked like a salamander, and the word *gerrymandering—Gerry* plus *salamander*—was born.

districts, and each of those districts will send a representative to the state legislature. In a perfect system, districts would be divided in such a way as to represent the political makeup of the state. In the example given here, then, three districts should have a green majority, whereas two districts would have a yellow majority.

Originally, redistricting occurred once every ten years after the census. In 2003, the Republican-led legislature decided to redistrict three years after the census had been completed. They had not redistricted three years earlier after the census. So legislators assumed they could still redistrict, as long as it was before the next census. Democrats took the case to the Supreme Court, which ruled the redistricting as legal. The court did find, however, that in one district, the minority vote was unfairly distributed and in violation of the Voting Rights Act of 1965. But the redistricting was allowed to stand, setting a precedent that gerrymandering was permitted.

But consider a case in which the green party has the majority of seats in the state legislature. During the next election, the green majority decides to make sure it has as many seats as possible. So it redraws the district lines in such a way that it gains more seats. The green party might "pack" those who vote for the yellow party into just two districts or "crack" a community of yellow voters into several different districts to dilute the effect of their votes. Both packing and cracking are gerrymandering techniques designed to give the green party an advantage. The oddly shaped districts that result from gerrymandering are not fair, and they don't provide an accurate representation of the political makeup of the state. But they do give green the majority in the election.

ALL THE WAY TO THE SUPREME COURT

Incidents of gerrymandering in states including Wisconsin and North Carolina were being reviewed by the Supreme Court in the summer of 2017. In Wisconsin, the Republican majority

Virginia was required to redraw district lines in 2014. The districts had been gerrymandered so that most of the black population was in a single district.

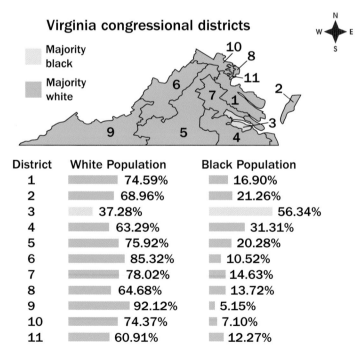

Virginia congressional districts

District	White Population	Black Population
1	74.59%	16.90%
2	68.96%	21.26%
3	37.28%	56.34%
4	63.29%	31.31%
5	75.92%	20.28%
6	85.32%	10.52%
7	78.02%	14.63%
8	64.68%	13.72%
9	92.12%	5.15%
10	74.37%	7.10%
11	60.91%	12.27%

gerrymandered the districts before the 2012 election, allowing Republicans to win one-third more state assembly seats, even though Democrats won the popular vote.

In North Carolina, where more Democrats are registered to vote than Republicans, the Supreme Court will decide on the partisan division of the state into ten Republican districts and three Democratic districts.[2] The state representative responsible for the gerrymandered districts seemed to think he hadn't gone far enough. If he could have found a way, he explained, he would have arranged it so the state was made up of 11 Republican districts and two Democratic districts.[3]

On March 10, 2017, federal judges ruled three Texas congressional districts void because they used race for partisan advantage. In another case, a San Antonio court found that legislators drew 2011 maps to diminish the effect of the minority vote.

But Republicans aren't the only party guilty of gerrymandering districts. In Maryland in 2011, a Democrat-controlled legislature redistricted specifically to ensure that a long-standing Republican congressman would lose his seat. And Maryland's third congressional district, home to Democratic congressman John Sarbanes, is the second-most gerrymandered district in the nation.[4]

In the state of Illinois, gerrymandering by the Democratic majority has led to a showdown between the parties over the state budget that has lasted from 2015 to 2017. Illinois governor Bruce Rauner, a Republican, is pushing for a bipartisan redistricting commission in the state. "We have our partisan-drawn maps so that there's no competition—and the politicians don't have to earn votes," Rauner said. "Two-thirds of the races for the General Assembly last November, there was no opponent. That's not democracy, that's a rigged system. And we should have redistricting reform in Illinois and across America."[5]

DON'T MESS WITH TEXAS

After the 2010 census, two states saw significant upticks in population—Florida and Texas. In Texas, the population grew by a whopping 4.3 million.[6] Because the number of seats a state holds in the House of Representatives depends on population, Texas was granted four new seats in the US Congress. More seats gives Texas a bigger voice in government. But although Texas is a state with a Republican majority, most of the 4.3 million people who moved to Texas before the last census were either Latino or African American, two groups that historically vote for Democrats. Republican lawmakers turned to redistricting to ensure the new seats went to the Republican majority. The end result was gerrymandering with no regard for the Voting Rights Act. As a result, in 2017 there were several Texas-related gerrymandering lawsuits under review in Texas district courts and the Supreme Court.

WHAT IS THE SOLUTION?

The United States is the only democracy in the world where legislators are involved in redistricting decisions. In Australia and the United Kingdom, nonpartisan commissions have been established to handle all redistricting. This might be an option

Chris Jankowski is one politician who has been accused of gerrymandering.

GERRYMANDERING GENIUS

Tom Hofeller has built a career out of gerrymandering districts, first for the Democratic Party and more recently for the Republican Party. Hofeller travels to states where redistricting is needed and coaches legislators on the do's and don'ts of redistricting. Essentially, his tips include following the law and keeping a low profile by using a secure server, using a safe phone or talking in person, and not e-mailing. Most importantly, Hofeller urges legislators to redistrict with moderation—resist the urge to pool too many pro-Republican precincts into one district. Being discreet is key. Hofeller typically gets results. With his help, Republicans were able to gain 721 seats in state legislatures in the 2010 election.[8] They held more than 4,100 of the 7,383 seats, enabling the party to take control of legislatures.[9]

for the United States—if legislators could set aside their political interests long enough to vote objectively on districting reform. In today's highly partisan climate, however, this seems unlikely.

Another option may be to create districts using a computer program. The Center for Range Voting developed the "shortest splitline algorithm," which divides states into districts with comparable populations using the straightest possible lines.[7] A second program, created by Brian Olson, arranges districts according to the shortest distance from voters to their polling centers.

But both of these programs have drawbacks. Although they develop districts that are unbiased and evenly populated, computer programs don't take into account a community's makeup. Cohesive neighborhoods with a shared set of beliefs may be broken up into different districts on computer-generated maps.

Perhaps the Supreme Court decisions in upcoming gerrymandering cases will provide an answer. The Supreme Court will be hearing cases on partisan gerrymandering in Wisconsin, North Carolina, and Maryland. In past cases, judges have claimed gerrymanders were harmful to the democratic process. Justice Anthony M. Kennedy made a key observation during a 2004 case: "The ordered working of our Republic, and of the democratic process, depends on a sense of decorum and restraint in all branches of government, and in the citizenry itself."[10] But the court had yet to strike down a gerrymander.

DISCUSSION STARTERS

- Why is it necessary to adjust voting districts after every government census?

- Do you think elected officials should be involved in the redistricting process? Why or why not?

- How do you think gerrymandering could be prevented?

CHAPTER 8

VOTING IN A CHANGING NATION

Adriano Espaillat, born in the Dominican Republic, took office in the House of Representatives in 2017.

Despite the many questions about voting rights in the United States, one thing is certain: the demographics of the nation are changing rapidly. It is projected that by 2055, the United States will not have a single ethnic or racial majority. White people, who made up 85 percent of the population in 1960, are projected to make up only 43 percent by 2060. At the same time, the percentage of Hispanics and African Americans will grow to 45 percent combined.[1] For the next 50 years, most new immigrants to the United States will come from Asian and Hispanic countries.

This population shift promises to shake up politics in the United States and shine a light on questions about voting rights. Already in 2016, the substantial increase in Hispanic voters made for the most diverse voting population in US history.

WHO VOTES?

In light of these projections, laws about who may vote will affect a higher percentage of the growing population. By current law, a person is eligible to vote in the United States if he or she meets the following criteria: is a US citizen by either birth or naturalization, meets the state's residency requirements, and is at least 18 years old.

Noncitizens, then, must go through the process of naturalization to be able to vote. This requirement affects many more people than one might think—today, 14 percent of the US population is foreign-born, and that number is projected

THE MILLENNIAL FACTOR

The increase in the percentage of the US population that is made up of millennials—Americans born after 1980—will alter the nation's electorate as well. Young adults in this age-group don't necessarily identify with any political party—in fact, 50 percent call themselves independents—but they tend to hold more liberal views than older Americans. Millennials are also more diverse than any generation in the past, with 43 percent of them being nonwhite people.[2]

to increase.[3] By 2065, immigrants are projected to make up 18 percent of the population.[4]

Many feel strongly that noncitizens should not be granted voting rights. These opponents argue that voting is a responsibility of citizenship. Those who are not willing to make the commitment to becoming citizens should not have a right to participate fully in the democratic process. But there are some who argue that noncitizens with a Lawful Permanent Resident card who work, pay taxes to the US government, and send their children to public schools should be eligible to vote. In early America, those who paid taxes could vote. After 1840, in fact, noncitizens had the right to vote in 40 states.[5]

Former felons pose another question. Some believe that former felons—those who have committed serious crimes such as murder, rape, armed robbery, or child molestation, but have served their time in prison—should not be allowed to vote at all. They believe former felons gave up their civil rights forever the moment they so severely infringed on the rights of their victims. Others believe preventing former felons from voting for the rest of their lives is extreme and unconstitutional. They believe former felons should be able to vote again, but only after a defined waiting period once they've been released from prison.

Just how voting rights are reinstated varies greatly between states. In all but two states—Maine and Vermont—those who've been convicted of a felony lose their right to vote while they are serving prison time. What happens once they are released from prison varies widely from state to state. In 38 states and the District of Columbia, voting rights are automatically restored to felons as soon as they have served their prison sentence. In other states, felons regain voting rights after a certain period of time once they are released from prison. And in nine states, felons must apply to have their voting rights restored. At the state level, legislation has been passed to try to streamline the process of restoring voting rights to former felons and to provide assistance navigating the voting registration process.

To further complicate the issue, the US

Henry Straight of Iowa hired a lawyer to try to get his right to vote reinstated but was still rejected.

criminal justice system disproportionately incarcerates African Americans. Black people are sent to prison more than five times more often than white people for the same offenses. Although African Americans and Latinos constitute 32 percent of the population, they made up 56 percent of those imprisoned in 2015.[6] These statistics, when combined with the challenges felons face in regaining voting rights, point to an increase in the number of African Americans who are disenfranchised.

ELECTORAL COLLEGE

Another voting question that's surfaced in recent years pertains to the electoral college. Many have argued that the electoral college is outdated and should be abolished. The electoral college is the process by which the president and vice president are elected to office. This system was created by the Founding Fathers in 1787 as a way to prevent political corruption and give states with fewer people more of a voice in the election process.

Every presidential election year, political parties hold state conventions in November to nominate electors. Electors are the representatives who will cast the official vote for the presidential and vice presidential candidates. The number of electors nominated from each state varies, but every state sends a number equal to the total senators (always two) plus the number of representatives it has. This means there are between three and 54 electors from each state, for a total of 538 electors.[7]

Voters go to the polls on the first Tuesday in November to cast a ballot for the presidential candidate of their choice. But voters are actually voting for the electors who have pledged to vote for the candidate in the electoral college. After the election, the electors gather in their home states on the Monday after the second Wednesday in December to vote. It is a "winner takes all" system, which means the candidate who wins the most votes in a state takes all the state's available electors.

The votes are counted and certified on January 6 in the year immediately following the election. To win the election, the president needs to have votes from at least 270 of the 538 electors.

VOTING REGISTRATION FOR FORMER FELONS

Once former felons have had their voting rights restored, registering to vote can be frustrating. Not only is there a great deal of paperwork to complete, but former felons also must gather documentation about the nature of their crime and the dates of their prison term and coordinate information between state agencies. Even with all these pieces in place, former felons may wait a long time before their reregistration is complete due to the backlog of such applications at understaffed agencies.

If no candidate wins the majority, the House of Representatives elects the president, and the Senate elects the vice president.

Most of the time, the candidate who wins the electoral college also wins the popular vote. But in 1824, 1876, 1888, 2000, and 2016, the candidates who won the popular vote lost in the electoral college, ultimately losing their bids for the presidency. Since the 2000 election, when Democratic candidate Al Gore won the popular vote but Republican candidate George W. Bush won the electoral college, there has been a debate about whether the electoral college should be eliminated.

THOSE FOR AND THOSE AGAINST

Those who wish to do away with the electoral college argue that the system steps on the "one person, one vote" premise of democracy. Critics also say that the existence of the electoral college pushes candidates to focus campaign efforts on winning over only those states with many votes that can bring them over the top in the college, while ignoring constituents in other states. They will also avoid states where the large majority consistently votes for one party.

Those who support the electoral college argue that it forces candidates to campaign in swing states, avoids runoff elections, and provides a more certain outcome, avoiding

2016 Presidential Election Electoral Votes

Democrats | Republicans

In the 2016 election, Donald Trump won 304 electoral votes while Hillary Clinton won 227.

recounts. A more certain outcome is nearly always guaranteed because with the winner-takes-all system, the winner's portion of electoral votes will always be more than his or her share of the popular vote.

If the electoral college didn't exist, candidates would limit their campaigning to areas with the most voters—mainly big cities and suburbs. By so doing, candidates might ignore the segment of the population in rural areas and fail to represent their interests. Electorates serve to give more weight to less-populous states. The electoral college also lessens the need for runoff elections. In the event that more than two candidates run and the winner of the popular vote doesn't have a clear majority, a runoff election between the top two candidates would be necessary.

AGAINST THE ELECTORAL COLLEGE

After the 2000 election, Hillary Clinton spoke out against the electoral college system. "I believe strongly that in a democracy, we should respect the will of the people, and to me that means it's time to do away with the electoral college and move to the popular election of our president."[9] Little did Clinton know at the time that 16 years later she would win the popular vote but lose the electoral college in her bid for the presidency against Donald Trump.

POSSIBLE SOLUTIONS

To do away with the electoral college completely would require an amendment to the Constitution, which is a difficult process. The group National Popular Vote is trying to find a way around the amendment process by passing laws that require electors in all states to vote for the candidate who wins the popular vote. Although ten states and the District of Columbia, which represent a total of 165 electoral votes, support this proposal, 270 electoral votes are needed for approval.[8]

Another option would be for states to abandon the winner-takes-all system and adopt a process similar to what is

Barry Fadem, *left*, president of National Popular Vote, worked with New Mexico's senate to promote the National Popular Vote bill.

used in Maine and Nebraska, where the electors are divided in proportion to vote totals in the state.

THE FUTURE

Many questions remain about the future of voting rights in the United States. For example, if the Supreme Court decides that partisan gerrymandering is unconstitutional, states must figure out how to ensure that districts are balanced and unbiased.

And if states continue to pass voter ID laws, they will need to reach a compromise that will guard against voter fraud yet provide nondiscriminatory voting rights to all who are eligible. There are questions about whether the electoral college should remain a part of the US election process and whether voting rights should be extended to noncitizens and former felons. The answers to these questions will have a profound effect on the voting rights of Americans for generations to come.

DISCUSSION STARTERS

- What does the right to vote mean to you? Explain your answer.

- Do you think noncitizens should be allowed to vote? Why or why not?

- In Vermont and Maine, felons are allowed to vote while they are serving prison time. Do you think this is a good idea or a bad idea? Why?

- Do you think the United States should get rid of the electoral college? Why or why not?

TIMELINE

1776

With the Declaration of Independence, states rewrite their constitutions to deny women the right to vote. Between 1776 and 1807, only women in the state of New Jersey who own property can vote.

1807

Male legislators officially outlaw women's suffrage.

1819

New states entering the Union after this date deny voting rights to all African Americans.

1848

The first Women's Rights Convention is held in Seneca Falls, New York, on July 19 and 20.

MID-1800s

Literacy tests begin to be imposed on voters.

1861–1865

During the American Civil War, women suspend work toward equal rights for women to support the abolitionist movement.

1869

Wyoming Territory grants women older than 21 years the right to vote.

1870

The Fifteenth Amendment passes, prohibiting states from denying a male citizen the right to vote based on race, color, or previous condition of servitude.

1880s

African-American men vote and hold office in many Southern states.

1890s

Former Confederate states take steps to ensure African Americans cannot vote by conducting literacy tests and passing grandfather clauses that prevented those whose ancestors had not been able to vote in the 1860s from voting in current elections.

1910–1918

Women gain the right to vote in 16 states.

1920

The Nineteenth Amendment passes, granting women the right to vote. African-American women in many Southern states, however, are disenfranchised through literacy tests, poll taxes, or grandfather clauses.

1950s

Some states use literacy tests to prevent African Americans from voting. Alabama, Arkansas, Mississippi, Texas, and Virginia charge a poll tax to keep African Americans from registering to vote. In Alabama, voters have to complete a written test on the Constitution and government to vote.

1957

The Civil Rights Act passes, allowing the US government to file suits in voting rights cases.

EARLY 1965

Martin Luther King Jr. begins a voter registration drive in Selma, Alabama, where disenfranchisement of African Americans is most prevalent.

MARCH 7, 1965

King calls for a march from Selma to the state capital of Montgomery in the name of voting rights.

AUGUST 6, 1965

The Voting Rights Act is signed into law.

JUNE 25, 2013

In a 5–4 vote, the Supreme Court overturns Section 4 of the Voting Rights Act, allowing affected states and jurisdictions freedom to adjust voting laws and districts without federal approval.

NOVEMBER 5, 2013

Texas becomes one of many states to pass a voter ID law in the wake of the overturning of Section 4.

ESSENTIAL FACTS

THE RIGHT TO VOTE

- The US Constitution gives all citizens the right to vote.

- The Fifteenth Amendment, passed in 1870, granted African-American men the right to vote.

- The Nineteenth Amendment, passed in 1920, granted women the right to vote.

LIMITATIONS

Throughout the history of the United States, the right to vote has been limited by grandfather clauses, poll taxes, literacy tests, voter ID laws, gerrymandering, and targeting race and gender.

KEY PLAYERS

- Carrie Chapman Catt was a leader in the American women's suffrage movement and president of the National American Woman Suffrage Association. She was instrumental in convincing President Woodrow Wilson to sign the Nineteenth Amendment, which granted women the right to vote.

- Elizabeth Cady Stanton was a women's rights activist and co-organizer of the first Women's Rights Convention in Seneca Falls in 1848.

- Frederick Douglass was a leading abolitionist and supporter of the women's rights movement who pushed for African Americans and women to have the right to vote.

- Lyndon B. Johnson was the 36th president of the United States. He signed the Voting Rights Act into law on August 6, 1965.

- Rev. Martin Luther King Jr. was a leader during the civil rights movement of the 1960s. He led the march from Selma to Montgomery on Bloody Sunday, March 7, 1965.

KEY PERSPECTIVES

- The right to vote is the foundation of people's ability to think for themselves and participate fully in the democratic process.

- If any part of society is denied the right to vote, the government itself is compromised.

- No person shall be kept from voting because of race or color.

- Frederick Douglass, referring to African Americans, said, "By depriving us of suffrage, you affirm our incapacity to form an intelligent judgment respecting public men and public measures; you declare before the world that we are unfit to exercise the elective franchise, and by this means lead us to undervalue ourselves, to put a low estimate upon ourselves, and to feel that we have no possibilities like other men."

- Woodrow Wilson wrote, "I agree without reservation that the full and sincere democratic reconstruction of the world for which we are striving, and which we are determined to bring about at any cost, will not have been completely or adequately attained until women are admitted to the suffrage."

- Voting is a responsibility of citizenship. Those who are not willing to make the commitment to becoming citizens should not have a right to participate fully in the democratic process.

QUOTE

"The ordered working of our Republic, and of the democratic process, depends on a sense of decorum and restraint in all branches of government, and in the citizenry itself."

—*Justice Anthony M. Kennedy, 2004*

GLOSSARY

ABOLITIONIST
A person who wants to end slavery.

BALLOT
A sheet of paper printed with the names of candidates running for office, on which voters mark their choice.

DEMOCRATIC PARTY
The political party that was in favor of slavery during Reconstruction, which has shifted to represent those with more liberal viewpoints.

DISCRIMINATION
Unfair treatment of other people, usually because of race, age, or gender.

DISENFRANCHISE
To deprive a group of a legal right.

ELECTOR
A member of the electoral college.

ELECTORAL COLLEGE
The collection of people who elect the president of the United States.

GERRYMANDER
To redistrict to give a distinct advantage to a particular political party.

GRANDFATHER CLAUSE
A clause in a law that allows exceptions to a new law based on past situations.

JURISDICTION
A political territory.

LYNCH
To kill someone illegally as punishment for a crime.

PLAINTIFF
The one accusing a defendant in a court of law.

PREJUDICE
An unfair feeling of dislike for a person or group because of race, sex, or religion.

PROVISIONAL
Temporary.

RATIFY
To formally approve or adopt an idea or document.

REDISTRICT
To alter the boundaries of voting districts to evenly distribute voters between them.

REPUBLICAN PARTY
A political party formed to oppose the spread of slavery in the United States, which now represents more conservative viewpoints.

SUFFRAGE
The right to vote in a political election.

VOTER ID LAW
A state law that requires a voter to present a state-issued ID to vote.

WHITE SUPREMACY
The belief that white people are superior to all other races.

ADDITIONAL RESOURCES

SELECTED BIBLIOGRAPHY

Fiffer, Steve. *Jimmie Lee & James: Two Lives, Two Deaths, and the Movement That Changed America*. New York: Regan Arts, 2015. Print.

Keyssar, Alexander. *The Right to Vote: The Contested History of Democracy in the United States*. New York: Basic, 2000. Print.

May, Gary. *Bending toward Justice: The Voting Rights Act and the Transformation of American Democracy*. New York: Basic, 2013. Print.

FURTHER READINGS

Cummings, Judy Dodge. *The Emancipation Proclamation*. Minneapolis, MN: Abdo, 2017. Print.

Freedman, Russell. *Because They Marched: The People's Campaign for Voting Rights That Changed America*. New York: Holiday, 2014. Print.

Lowery, Lynda Blackmon. *Turning 15 on the Road to Freedom: My Story of the 1965 Selma Voting Rights March*. New York: Dial, 2015. Print.

ONLINE RESOURCES

Booklinks
NONFICTION NETWORK
FREE! ONLINE NONFICTION RESOURCES

To learn more about the right to vote, visit **abdobooklinks.com**. These links are routinely monitored and updated to provide the most current information available.

MORE INFORMATION

For more information on this subject, contact or visit the following organizations:

IDA B. WELLS-BARNETT MUSEUM

220 N. Randolph Street
Holly Springs, MS 38635
662-252-3232

idabwellsmuseum.org

Located at the Spires Bolling House in Holly Springs, where Ida B. Wells was born, the Ida B. Wells-Barnett Museum features African-American culture displays and details about Wells-Barnett's life.

NATIONAL VOTING RIGHTS MUSEUM AND INSTITUTE

6 US Highway 80 East
Selma, AL 36701
334-526-4640

nvrmi.com

Located at the base of the Edmund Pettus Bridge in Selma, Alabama, this museum honors and remembers the stories of those who fought for voting rights during the civil rights movement.

WOMEN'S RIGHTS NATIONAL HISTORIC PARK

136 Fall Street
Seneca Falls, NY 13148
315-568-0024

nps.gov/wori/planyourvisit/basicinfo.htm

At this park in Seneca Falls, visitors can tour key sites of the first Women's Rights Convention, including the Wesleyan Chapel, where the convention took place, and Elizabeth Cady Stanton's home, which she called the "Center of the Rebellion."

SOURCE NOTES

CHAPTER 1. THE MARCH FROM SELMA TO MONTGOMERY

1. "Selma-to-Montgomery March: National Historic Trail & All-American Road." *National Park Service.* US Department of the Interior, n.d. Web. 16 Aug. 2017.

2. Steve Fiffer. *Jimmie Lee & James: Two Lives, Two Deaths, and the Movement That Changed America.* New York: Regan Arts, 2015. Print. 79.

3. "Selma, Alabama (Bloody Sunday, March 7, 1965)." *BlackPast.org.* BlackPast.org, 2017. Web. 16 Aug. 2017.

4. "Today in History—March 7." *Library of Congress.* Congress.gov, n.d. Web. 16 Aug. 2017.

5. Ibid.

6. Steven Mintz. "Winning the Vote: A History of Voting Rights." *History Now.* Gilder Lehrman Institute of American History, n.d. Web. 16 Aug. 2017.

7. "President Johnson's Special Message to the Congress: The American Promise." *LBJ Presidential Library.* LBJ Presidential Library, 15 Mar. 1965. Web. 16 Aug. 2017.

CHAPTER 2. VOTING IN EARLY AMERICA

1. Ed Crews. "Voting in Early America." *CW Journal.* Colonial Williamsburg, 2007. Web. 16 Aug. 2017.

2. "What the Black Man Wants." *Frederick Douglass Heritage.* Frederick Douglass Heritage, n.d. Web. 16 Aug. 2017.

3. "Frederick Douglass and the Abolitionist Movement." *Frederick Douglass Heritage.* Frederick Douglass Heritage, n.d. Web. 16 Aug. 2017.

4. "Black Codes." *History.* A&E Television Networks, 2017. Web. 16 Aug. 2017.

5. "Fifteenth Amendment." *History.* A&E Television Networks, 2017. Web. 16 Aug. 2017.

CHAPTER 3. WOMEN'S SUFFRAGE

1. "Seneca Falls Convention Begins." *History.* A&E Television Networks, 2017. Web. 16 Aug. 2017.

2. "Report of the Woman's Rights Convention." *Women's Rights: National Historic Park New York.* National Park Service, 26 Feb. 2015. Web. 16 Aug. 2017.

3. Rebecca Price. "5 Things You May Not Know about the Seneca Falls Convention." *Huffington Post.* Huffington Post, 17 July 2015. Web. 16 Aug. 2017.

4. "Suffragist Alice Paul Clashed with Woodrow Wilson." *American Experience.* PBS, 2017. Web. 16 Aug. 2017.

5. "Today in History—August 28." *Library of Congress*. Congress.gov, n.d. Web. 17 Aug. 2017.

6. "Carrie Chapman Catt (1859–1947)." *Carrie Chapman Catt Center for Women and Politics*. Iowa State University, 2017. Web. 17 Aug. 2017.

7. "Letter from President Wilson to Catt, June 7, 1918." *Iowa State University*. Iowa State University, 7 June 1918. Web. 16 Aug. 2017.

8. "19th Amendment." *History*. A&E Television Networks, 2017. Web. 16 Aug. 2017.

CHAPTER 4. CIVIL RIGHTS MOVEMENT

1. Barbara Bair. *Though Justice Sleeps: African Americans 1880–1900*. New York: Oxford, 1997. 60. *Google Books*. Web. 17 Aug. 2017.

2. Karlson Yu. "Springfield Race Riot, 1908." *BlackPast.org*. BlackPast.org, 2017. Web. 16 Aug. 2017.

3. "Fanny Lou Hammer." *American Experience*. PBS, 2017. Web. 16 Aug. 2017.

4. Howard Zinn. "On the Road to Voting Rights: Freedom Day in Selma, 1963." *HowardZinn.org*. HowardZinn.org, 30 Dec. 2014. Web. 16 Aug. 2017.

5. "Freedom Summer." *History*. A&E Television Networks, 2017. Web. 16 Aug. 2017.

6. Steven Mintz. "Winning the Vote: A History of Voting Rights. *History Now*. Gilder Lehrman Institute of American History, 2017. Web. 16 Aug. 2017.

CHAPTER 5. UPHOLDING THE VOTING RIGHTS ACT

1. "Race and Voting in the Segregated South." *Constitutional Rights Foundation*. Constitutional Rights Foundation, 2017. Web. 16 Aug. 2017.

2. Ibid.

3. "Final 2016 Election Results." *Selma Times-Journal*. Selma Times-Journal, 2016. Web. 16 Aug. 2017.

4. "History of Federal Voting Rights Laws." *US Department of Justice*. US Department of Justice, 28 July 2017. Web. 16 Aug. 2017.

5. Sam Roberts. "2008 Surge in Black Voters Nearly Erased Racial Gap." *New York Times*. New York Times, 20 July 2009. Web. 16 Aug. 2017.

6. Ibid.

7. Seth Stephens-Davidowitz. "How Racist Are We? Ask Google." *New York Times*. New York Times, 9 June 2012. Web. 16 Aug. 2017.

8. Jeffrey Toobin. "Casting Votes." *New Yorker*. Condé Nast, 14 Jan. 2013. Web. 16 Aug. 2017.

SOURCE NOTES CONTINUED

9. Ryan J. Reilly et al. "Voting Rights Act Section 4 Struck Down by Supreme Court." *Huffington Post*. Huffington Post, 25 June 2013. Web. 16 Aug. 2017.

10. Ari Berman. "Supreme Court: Uphold the Voting Rights Act!" *The Nation*. The Nation, 6 Mar. 2013. Web. 16 Aug. 2017.

11. Ibid.

12. "Supreme Court Strikes Down Section 4 of the Voting Rights Act." *PBS NewsHour Extra*. NewsHour, 25 June 2013. Web. 17 Aug. 2017.

13. Ari Berman. "Supreme Court: Uphold the Voting Rights Act!" *The Nation*. The Nation, 6 Mar. 2013. Web. 16 Aug. 2017.

CHAPTER 6. VOTER ID LAWS

1. Margaret Menge. "Researcher Claims Millions of Non-Citizens Voting in US Elections." *PoliZette*. Ingraham Media, 7 July 2017. Web. 17 Aug. 2017.

2. Pam Zekman. "2 Investigators: Chicago Voters Cast Ballots from Beyond the Grave." *CBS Chicago*. CBS Broadcasting, 27 Oct. 2016. Web. 17 Aug. 2017.

3. Max Siegelbaum. "Colorado Investigating Potential Fraud after News Report of 'Dead Voters.'" *Denver Post*. Digital First, 23 Sept. 2016. Web. 17 Aug. 2017.

4. Christina A. Cassidy and Ivan Moreno. "Voter ID Law Proved Insurmountable for Many in Wisconsin." *Wisconsin State Journal*. Wisconsin State Journal, 9 May 2017. Web. 17 Aug. 2017.

5. Zoltan L. Hajnal, Nazita Lajevardi, and Lindsay Nielson. "Do Voter Identification Laws Suppress Minority Voting? Yes. We Did the Research." *Washington Post*. Washington Post, 15 Feb. 2017. Web. 17 Aug. 2017.

6. Jasmine C. Lee. "How States Moved toward Stricter Voter ID Laws." *New York Times*. New York Times, 3 Nov. 2016. Web. 17 Aug. 2017.

7. Ari Berman. "Wisconsin's Voter-ID Law Suppressed 200,000 Votes in 2016 (Trump Won by 22,748)." *The Nation*. The Nation, 9 May 2017. Web. 17 Aug. 2017.

CHAPTER 7. GERRYMANDERING

1. Michael Wines. "Key Question for Supreme Court: Will It Let Gerrymanders Stand?" *New York Times*. New York Times, 21 Apr. 2017. Web. 17 Aug. 2017.

2. "Supreme Court Strikes Down 2 NC Congressional Districts." *Fox News Politics*. Fox News, 22 May 2017. Web. 17 Aug. 2017.

3. Erin Jensen. "John Oliver Tackles Gerrymandering, Advocates for EDM Bros, SantaCon Attendees." *USA Today*. USA Today, 10 Apr. 2017. Web. 17 Aug. 2017.

4. Christopher Ingraham. "America's Most Gerrymandered Congressional Districts." *Washington Post*. Washington Post, 15 May 2016. Web. 17 Aug. 2017.

5. Jason Rosenbaum. "On the Trail: Illinois Democrats Guard District-Drawing Privileges." *St. Louis Public Radio*. St. Louis Public Radio, 23 Apr. 2017. Web. 17 Aug. 2017.

6. Robert Draper. "The League of Dangerous Mapmakers." *Atlantic*. Atlantic, Oct. 2012. Web. 17 Aug. 2017.

7. "Gerrymandering—Proving All Politics Is Local." *Politics & Policy*. Politics & Policy, n.d. Web. 17 Aug. 2017.

8. Tim Storey. "GOP Makes Historic State Legislative Gains in 2010." *Rasmussen Reports*. Rasmussen Reports, 10 Dec. 2010. Web. 17 Aug. 2017.

9. "NCSL's The Canvass." *NCSL*. NCSL, Oct. 2016. Web. 17 Aug. 2017.

10. Michael Wines. "Key Question for Supreme Court: Will It Let Gerrymanders Stand?" *New York Times*. New York Times, 21 Apr. 2017. Web. 17 Aug. 2017.

CHAPTER 8. VOTING IN A CHANGING NATION

1. Danielle Restuccia. "A Study on the Changing Racial Makeup of 'The Next America.'" *Huffington Post*. Huffington Post, 23 June 2014. Web. 17 Aug. 2017.

2. D'Vera Cohn and Andrea Caumont. "10 Demographic Trends That Are Shaping the US and the World." *Fact Tank: News in the Numbers*. Pew Research Center, 31 Mar. 2016. Web. 17 Aug. 2017.

3. Ibid.

4. "Chapter 2: Immigration's Impact on Past and Future US Population Change." *Pew Research Center: Hispanic Trends*. Pew Research Center, 28 Sept. 2015. Web. 17 Aug. 2017.

5. "Should Non-Citizens in the US Vote?" *Los Angeles Times*. Los Angeles Times, 21 Dec. 2014. Web. 17 Aug. 2017.

6. "Criminal Justice Fact Sheet." *NAACP*. NAACP, 2017. Web. 17 Aug. 2017.

7. "What Is the Electoral College?" *US Electoral College*. US Electoral College, n.d. Web. 17 Aug. 2017.

8. "Keep the Electoral College: Our View." *USA Today*. USA Today, 10 Nov. 2016. Web. 17 Aug. 2017.

9. Jonathan Mahler and Steve Eder. "The Electoral College Is Hated by Many. So Why Does It Endure?" *New York Times*. New York Times, 10 Nov. 2016. Web. 17 Aug. 2017.

INDEX

ABOUT THE AUTHORS

DUCHESS HARRIS, JD, PHD

Professor Harris is the chair of the American Studies Department at Macalester College. The author and coauthor of four books (*Hidden Human Computers: The Black Women of NASA* and *Black Lives Matter* with Sue Bradford Edwards, *Racially Writing the Republic: Racists, Race Rebels, and Transformations of American Identity* with Bruce Baum, and *Black Feminist Politics from Kennedy to Clinton/Obama*), she has been an associate editor for *Litigation News*, the American Bar Association Section's quarterly flagship publication, and was the first editor-in-chief of *Law Raza Journal*, an interactive online race and the law journal for William Mitchell College of Law.

She has earned a PhD in American Studies from the University of Minnesota and a Juris Doctorate from William Mitchell College of Law.

KARI A. CORNELL

Kari A. Cornell is a writer and editor who loves to read, garden, cook, run, and craft. She is the author of the award-winning book *The Nitty-Gritty Gardening Book: Fun Projects for All Seasons* and many other histories, biographies, and cookbooks for kids. She lives in Minneapolis, Minnesota, with her husband, two sons, and her crazy dog, Emmylou.